SURVIVOR STORIES™

HURRICANE

True Stories of Survival

Philip Wolny

rosen publishing's
rosen central®

New York

For my grandfather, Jan Hetlof

Published in 2007 by The Rosen Publishing Group, Inc.
29 East 21st Street, New York, NY 10010

First Edition

Library of Congress Cataloging-in-Publication Data

Wolny, Philip.
Hurricane : true stories of survival / Philip Wolny. — 1st ed.
p. cm. — (Survivor stories)
Includes bibliographical references and index.
ISBN-13: 978-1-4042-0998-5
ISBN-10: 1-4042-0998-0 (library binding)
1. Hurricanes. 2. Survival skills. I. Title.
HV635.5.W65 2007
363.34'92–dc22

2006018916

Printed in China

On the cover: Rescuers guide Orleans parish residents stranded by Hurricane Katrina's floods to safety in New Orleans, Louisiana, on August 30, 2005. Emergency workers helped save many lives after the most destructive hurricane in U.S. history.

CONTENTS

This true-color image of Hurricane Ivan was captured by satellite on September 16, 2004, as the storm moved over the southeastern United States. Modern technology aids scientists and the media in tracking dangerous and destructive storms.

INTRODUCTION: NATURE'S FURY

The word "disaster" brings a variety of images to mind. Disasters can be man-made, like a plane crash or terrorist attack. Natural disasters occur when nature collides with humanity. Regardless of how it occurs, a disaster's destructive force brings loss of life and property. Those who make it out alive may experience great joy at surviving. Still, there is the terrible pain of losing loved ones. Whole communities, and even nations, are affected by a disaster for years after the event.

There are few words that strike as much fear into the hearts of people as the word "hurricane." The word comes from the West Indian "hurakan," or "big wind." Hurricanes are large storms that form over warm ocean water in the Atlantic Ocean. Powerful winds spiral around a calm area in the eye, or center, of the storm. Hurricanes typically bring great amounts of rain. Their winds also push the ocean ahead of them, creating a wall of water called a storm surge.

Hurricane season in the Atlantic occurs between June and November. Hurricanes begin as tropical storms near Africa and gather moisture as they travel west. The more warm water they absorb from

In the aftermath of 2005's Hurricane Katrina, a useless evacuation sign sits in New Orleans, Louisiana, floodwaters.

the ocean, the more powerful they become. Once the winds hit 74 miles per hour (119 kilometers per hour), the storm is officially a hurricane. Storms have been recorded as packing winds as fast as 200 mph (322 km/h).

The Saffir-Simpson Hurricane Scale measures hurricanes on a scale of 1 to 5, according to their wind speed. The weakest hurricanes are Category 1 storms, and have winds between 74 and 95 mph (119 to 153 km/h). The strongest, Category 5 storms, have winds of 156 mph (251 km/h) or greater.

The energy in a hurricane is tremendous. Some scientists estimate that the average storm creates the same amount of energy as that of a ten-megaton atomic bomb that explodes every twenty minutes. When this fierce energy crashes into civilization, it is a recipe for disaster. The wind, storm surge, and rain can cause tremendous damage. Cars can be tossed like toys, trees uprooted, and buildings left in ruins. It is not uncommon for a hurricane to destroy houses, towns, and even whole cities.

Hurricanes can cause death or injuries in many different ways. People may drown from the storm surge or heavy flooding. Powerful winds can turn debris into dangerous missiles. A storm can also kill indirectly by cutting off access to valuable resources. Water, food, and electricity may become unavailable, sometimes for long periods of time. If someone is seriously injured, it can take far longer than normal for help to arrive.

Sometimes, government officials order people to evacuate before a hurricane hits. Those who leave may return to find their homes destroyed. For those who choose to stay, or cannot leave, it is often an experience they never forget. Their stories of survival remind us of the enormous power of nature and the strength of the human spirit.

1

HURRICANE ANDREW

For those who live along the Gulf Coast and eastern seaboard of the United States, hurricanes are a fact of life. Residents of Florida, the state most threatened by hurricanes, always fear that the "big one" will hit. In August 1992, that fear became a reality. On August 22, the National Hurricane Center (NHC) announced that a tropical storm passing through the Caribbean had reached hurricane strength. It was a small but powerful storm. Hurricane Andrew, as it came to be called, was headed for south Florida.

Getting Out

Hundreds of thousands of people evacuated. In Dade County alone, which includes Miami, about 517,000 fled. However, thousands more remained to ride out the storm. Many crowded into shelters, but others stayed in their homes. Residents hunkered down, waiting for the storm to hit.

Andrew made landfall around 4:30 AM on Monday, August 24. It had weakened slightly to a Category 4 storm, with winds gusting from about 140 to 175 mph (225 to 282 km/h). By 8 AM, the storm had moved across the tip of Florida and was on its way out to the Gulf of Mexico. The destruction left behind was immense, covering an area about the size of the city of Chicago. About 80,000 homes were badly damaged or destroyed. In a few short hours, Dade County looked as if it had been through a nuclear blast. For those who experienced the hurricane first-hand, those hours seemed like an eternity.

The View from Ground Zero

Stan Goldenberg was no stranger to hurricanes. As a meteorologist with the National Oceanic and Atmospheric Administration's (NOAA) Hurricane Research Division, he had flown into them many times. This time, however, he would experience the storm from the ground.

Goldenberg's wife had given birth to their fourth child the day before the storm, so he had had little time to prepare their Miami home before Hurricane Andrew struck. Neighbors had helped him nail some plywood on his windows. With his sons and his sister's family in the house, the three adults and six children braced themselves. When the storm hit, the plywood ripped off the living room window, and the glass shattered. They decided to seek refuge in the station wagon in

After the hurricane, a resident in Miami, Florida, stares out from his wall-less apartment *(bottom right)* on August 25, 1992.

the garage, but found that the main garage door was already gone. Being exposed to the wind, even inside a car, seemed risky. With nowhere else to go, they settled on the kitchen floor.

Goldenberg suddenly felt something heavy hit him in the back. His brother-in-law yelled that the roof was gone, as was the kitchen wall. The stove had landed on Goldenberg. Although he was in pain, he soon realized that the crumbled wall had created a protective barrier. It was little consolation, however. Rainwater was filling the house, the wind was bearing down on them, and the entire family was praying and screaming.

When the winds died down a little, the family was able to leave the ruined kitchen. In the end, the car seemed like the best prospect for safety. Crowding into it, they covered themselves with a carpet in case the windshield or windows shattered. They were shocked when they saw a neighbor wading through knee-deep water to them. His house had stayed mostly intact, and he invited them over.

They spent the rest of the storm there. Goldenberg's feet were numb for the next few months, but the family had escaped. His wife, Barbara, had spent the night in the hospital with their newborn child. She had seen the destruction on television and feared the worst. Both of them burst into tears when he finally made it to the hospital.

Goldenberg was more in awe of the power of hurricanes. He felt he had learned a lesson, too. Even as an experienced meteorologist, he had not prepared properly. How many others who didn't have his knowledge of hurricanes had suffered like he had? Or worse?

Stan Goldenberg poses in front of the wreckage of his family's house. Hurricane Andrew tore off the roof and demolished the home while the Goldenberg family scrambled for shelter within.

The World Blown Away

Farther south, in the small city of Homestead, Florida, April Counts, like many people in the area, lived in a trailer. Counts had been listening to the radio, trying to find out where a local shelter was. She didn't realize that there were none; she had missed an evacuation order.

Not long after the winds had reached a deafening roar, the trailer began to shake and come apart. Struggling to help her roommate, a disabled veteran, Counts led the way out to her car. They curled up on the backseat floor. Counts was petrified that a tree would crush them, and was amazed to be alive in the morning. Everywhere she looked, there was wreckage.

Although grateful to be alive, Counts was angry that looters had stolen belongings from the ruins of her trailer. The thefts made her feel even more traumatized. Her home destroyed, she lived in Tent City, a massive shelter built in Homestead for the victims of Andrew. The goodwill and generosity she felt at the shelter, especially from U.S. Marines stationed there, restored some of her faith in humanity. She was thankful for a place to sleep and food to eat.

Caught by Surprise

Dan Sanabria, also in Homestead, Florida, was oblivious to the coming storm. He had spent the weekend moving from his mobile home to a

After Hurricane Andrew devastated southeastern Florida, the federal government dispatched U.S. Marines to help construct temporary shelter for those in need. This image, taken August 31, 1992, shows the tents set up in Homestead, Florida, for the thousands of residents left homeless.

house he would share with his elderly parents. Exhausted, he fell asleep late Sunday night, only to be awoken by the howling wind and strange noises before dawn. Investigating, he found the sliding-glass door moving in and out and the backyard shed moving up and down.

Like many people caught in a hurricane, Sanabria and his parents sought out the smallest room in the house for refuge: the bathroom. Sanabria braced himself against the door, and they tried to wait out Andrew's fury. A moment of calm arrived; they were in the eye of the storm. When Sanabria came out of the bathroom, he found that their roof was gone. Three minutes after they left the bathroom, the ceiling caved in. Like Stan Goldenberg, Sanabria and his family were lucky to make it to a neighbor's house.

Right after the storm, Sanabria drove by the mobile home he had just moved out of. The only thing left standing was the toilet. All but nine of the 1,176 trailers in Homestead had been destroyed.

PICKING UP THE PIECES

Andrew's path of destruction left 175,000 people homeless and was responsible for forty-three deaths in Florida. Those affected took shelter in tent cities or with relatives or friends. Thousands lined up for food, water, and medical care. The storm caused more than $30 billion in damage. Many survivors had to choose between moving away or rebuilding.

2

HURRICANE MITCH

Andrew was the most destructive hurricane to hit Florida in decades. Despite the hardships endured by south Floridians for years after, the hurricane hit a state in the most prosperous nation on Earth. Poorer nations, which have fewer resources to prepare for (and rebuild after) a disaster, often have a more difficult road to recovery. For Central Americans in the autumn of 1998, the "big one" would eclipse even Andrew's path of devastation.

In early October, Hurricane Mitch formed as a tropical disturbance off the shores of the Ivory Coast in Africa. Ten days later, it had traveled across the Atlantic and became a hurricane on October 24. Though it stayed far out at sea for a time, it grew in strength, packing 180 mph (290 km/h) winds. By the afternoon of Monday, October 26, the storm bore down on the islands north of Honduras. With idyllic beaches and coral reefs, the area is a popular destination for scuba divers and other tourists. Native Hondurans and vacationers alike would spend the next three days facing a monstrous ordeal.

A Dream Job Becomes a Sudden Nightmare

Hurricane Mitch kept moving in unexpected directions. By the time residents knew the storm was going to hit the island of Guanaja, it was only a few hours away. Most people, therefore, had little choice but to brave the storm on the island.

For the workers at the Bayman Bay Club on Guanaja, the last thing on their minds was facing nature's wrath. Chris and Alice Norris had just left their jobs in Rochester, New York, to become managers at the diving resort on the island's western shore. On Monday morning, October 26, Chris Norris woke his wife to tell her that a hurricane was six hours away. With winds of 155 mph (249 km/h), it was a Category 4 storm.

Luckily, the resort's owners had built two concrete bunkers under the resort. The managers decided to have the guests pile into one bunker with them, and the staff into the other bunker with their families. They prepared supplies and barricaded the bunkers' windows. By Monday evening, the winds had picked up to about 80 mph (129 km/h) on the island. When Mitch hit, the sound of the wind was deafening. Water was leaking in onto the floor, and the bunkers' occupants endured a hot, uncomfortable, and fearful night. The next day, when the storm had died down a bit, Chris Norris and another manager looked outside. They saw that winds had lifted and destroyed many of the resort's cabins.

An aerial photograph shows the island of Guanaja after the hurricane. Chris Norris and the owner of the Bayman Bay Club *(inset)* confer in front of the devastated resort.

Rescues Through the Night

The following night, one of the manager's wives realized that Ernesto, a new cook, was missing. Norris braved the winds and went outside to find him. He found the cook in 3 inches (7.6 cm) of water, hiding under his bed in his ruined cabin. The walls were crumbling and the roof was close to flying off.

He helped Ernesto out, and with a rope tied to them, the men struggled against the wind. They ran from one spot to another, dodging flying tree branches. Sometimes they would have to tie themselves to a tree stump or other object, lie flat on their stomachs, and wait out the strongest gusts. When they made it back to the staff bunker, Norris got Ernesto in and spent an hour returning to the other bunker, a distance of only 600 feet (183 meters).

Norris soon found himself facing the storm again. His wife feared that the kerosene lamps the staff was using in their airtight bunker would eventually suffocate them. On the way over, he had just barely tied himself to a tree trunk when the wind picked him up and held him flailing in the air. When he came back down to the ground, he made it to the staff bunker. He found everyone there passed out. Blowing out the lamps, he roused the staff.

By Friday, Hurricane Mitch had passed over Guanaja. With one-third of all homes destroyed and most trees on the island stripped of their leaves, Mitch had left its mark. Miraculously, only seven people perished. The Norrises were stunned, however. They had come there only a few days before and now their new life had almost literally blown away. Despite the storm, Chris and Alice Norris decided to stay at the Bayman Bay Club. Months later, they were still there, helping to rebuild. They counted their blessings: they had their health and were still living in a tropical paradise. Chris Norris said, "I still wonder sometimes, 'Why us?' But then, nobody died here—and next to that, what else matters?"

A Watery Grave

For the rest of Honduras, Mitch's terrible story had just begun. By Thursday, the storm started to move southeast toward the northern coast. With its diminished winds, Mitch was barely a hurricane when it made landfall. But it was no less deadly. Unlike Andrew, in which the deaths were mainly from wind, the greatest danger during Mitch was the unending rainfall.

Dumping as much as 2 feet (0.6 m) of rain in two days, Mitch devastated Honduras. The rivers and creeks that crisscross the mountainous country swelled to many times their normal size. The flooding caused mudslides that buried homes and wiped out whole villages and towns. Some residents on the Honduran coast were trapped between two brutal forces: the storm surge from the ocean, and the flooding from inland rivers. In one coastal region, the Aguan River spilled for miles outside of its regular course.

Stuck at Sea

In the village of Barra de Aguan, a schoolteacher, Laura Arriola, fled to a neighbor's roof with her family when their home was washed away. But the neighbor's house did not last much longer. Arriola, her husband, and their three children were swept into the water. Grabbing on to one son, she yelled for her husband to hold on to the other two. She soon lost sight of them. The water was powerful and before long, tore her son from her grip. She tried swimming after him, but could not find him. She then realized that she had been pulled out to sea. She was completely alone.

Arriola kept afloat by holding on to nearby palm branches. There was so much debris in the water that she was able to make a raft from branches, wood, and tree roots. Rough seas would knock her off the

Laura Arriola lost her family during Hurricane Mitch and barely escaped with her life after being dragged out to sea for days. Three weeks after being released from the hospital, her physical injuries were mostly healed, but the emotional ones lingered.

raft, but each time, she struggled back on. She lived on pineapples, oranges, and the milk from a coconut. The hours passed, and day turned into night. She cried and prayed for rescue, but none came.

Six days later, Arriola was still adrift when she looked up and saw a plane. She waved frantically. She even took off her black shirt, thinking they might more easily notice her red bra. The plane passed again and dropped something in the water near her. A half hour later, she realized it was a marker. A helicopter from the British vessel the HMS *Sheffield* then thundered over her. The British had been part of the relief effort on the mainland. A crewman descended and scooped her to safety.

Arriola had drifted 50 miles (80 km) from the shore. Tired, dehydrated, cold, and suffering from sun exposure, she was amazed to be alive. The rest of her family wasn't as fortunate. The bodies of her husband and daughter were soon found; her sons are missing and presumed dead.

FAR FROM HOME

Farther inland, water and earth mixed with terrifying results on Friday night. The small town of Concepción de María, near the border of Nicaragua, had already experienced daily rain for two weeks. From that Monday on, it had fallen nonstop. The earth could not absorb any more water and began to come apart. Landslides buried entire houses.

Others were cast down the steep hillsides or submerged by floods. Between the water, mud, and moving earth, it seemed as if the town was under attack.

In nearby Barrio Pedro Diaz, Santo Agripino Sanchez and his brothers-in-law barely had time to get out of their houses before the Choluteca River overran them. They all tried to climb onto Sanchez's roof, but his brothers-in-law were not fast enough. He saw them carried

Residents of the Honduran capital city of Tegucigalpa watch the raging floodwaters of the Choluteca River on October 31, 1998. Mitch brought torrential rains that claimed thousands of lives and destroyed much of the country's buildings and infrastructure.

away by the surging waves. Not long after, Sanchez's roof tipped over and he fell into the water, too. The water was so fast and strong, it was tearing most of the biggest trees out of the ground. Swept downstream, with logs crashing into him, he fought to keep his head above water.

On Saturday morning, Sanchez was still fighting for his life in the floodwaters. Bodies of people and animals and the remains of houses surrounded him. It was nearly afternoon when he was washed onto a patch of high ground. Stranded there for three days, Sanchez was finally picked up by a passing rescue team in a motorboat. They dropped him off twenty miles from home. Hitchhiking and walking, it took him another day to make it back to town. After five days, his family members who had survived embraced him tearfully. But he was shocked to see that the entire town had been destroyed.

A REGION DEVASTATED

Many people in Central America were caught off guard by the way Mitch first stalled off the coast while it poured heavy rains on the nation. Previous hurricanes had rarely moved inland like Mitch had. In Honduras and its neighboring countries, Mitch is estimated to have taken 11,000 lives, but many believe the actual number is higher. In Honduras alone, the official toll was 5,600 dead and 8,000 missing.

3

HURRICANE FLOYD

For North Carolina, the disastrous end of the 1999 hurricane season was weeks in the making. Hurricane Dennis had hit the eastern part of the state over the Labor Day weekend. It unleashed anywhere from 3 to 19 inches (8 to 48 cm) of rain throughout the state over the course of a week. The rain filled rivers and creeks, and the soil absorbed a great deal of water. Thunderstorms in the weeks after only added to the rising waters. Dennis had set the stage for a catastrophe of tragic proportions.

Hurricane Floyd followed closely on Dennis's heels. Its wind speeds were up to 155 mph (249 km/h) by September 13, when it lay 300 miles (483 km) east of the Bahamas. As powerful as Hurricane Andrew, Hurricane Floyd was nearly three times its size. From Florida up the eastern seaboard, nearly three million people evacuated ahead of the storm.

After brushing by Florida, Floyd made its way toward North Carolina, its winds down to 110 mph (177 km/h). The hurricane made landfall at Cape Fear, North Carolina, at 3 AM on September 16. In those early morning hours, winds, rising tides, and even a few tornados plagued the coast. But, like Hurricane Mitch, it was the rain that hit the hardest. With its waterways saturated from Dennis, North Carolina was not capable of handling another sixty hours of rain. Single-day rainfall records were broken, then broken again. The town of Wilmington, for example, got 19 inches (about half a meter) in twenty-four hours.

Flash floods, moving quickly and silently, surprised many victims. Some only realized they were in danger when rising water invaded their homes and, touching their skin, woke them. Rivers had overrun their banks. Creeks measuring only a few dozen feet across were now a mile wide. Familiar landscapes were unrecognizable.

HELP FROM ABOVE

Neither boats nor land vehicles could reach certain areas. So for many survivors, airborne evacuations were the only way out. In Greenville, seventeen-year-old Derek Latham climbed onto the roof of his home with his mother and two sisters. Floodwaters had filled their house and were now rising at their feet. They were starting to panic.

Soon, a Navy helicopter hovered into view. Because of trees surrounding the house, it could not land directly on the roof, as it did in other rescues. Instead, the Navy airmen were lowered into the water. They swam and scooped up the stranded family, securing them into rescue baskets, and lifted them to safety.

Derek Latham poses with family and an HC-2 helicopter rescue crew shortly after joining the U.S. Navy.

Latham was awed by their professionalism, which helped calm his family. "They were really shook up before, but when the crew landed, I saw the relief on their faces," he told the *Virginian-Pilot*. In fact, Latham was so affected by his family's rescue that he decided to join the Navy, specifically to become a rescue swimmer. "I wanted to join so that when I land and get out of the helicopter, people feel safe knowing that I will take care of them."

TREACHEROUS ROADS

Other rescuers had their hands full dealing with the flooded roads. Many victims were caught by surprise while driving. They did not realize the depths of the flooding, or the power of the water—just 2 feet (about half a meter) of water was strong enough to carry away a car. Ditches next to roads became invisible traps.

Gary Williams, fifteen years old, was traveling with his stepfather, Mitchell Piner, in a pickup truck outside the town of Wallace, North

Carolina. They were swept off the road and smashed into a tree by the rushing waters of an overflowing creek. Williams and Piner escaped through the back window. They could barely keep their heads above water, however, and were soon separated.

For Williams, luck arrived in the form of Erasmo Mencias. Mencias had seen the truck crash and heard the passengers' cries for help. The fifty-one-year-old construction worker dove into the water and found Williams. Grabbing the boy, he dragged him through the water to a tree. They held on until members of the Wallace Volunteer Fire

A pickup truck *(upper left)* braves dangerous floodwaters near Rocky Mount, North Carolina, on September 16, 1999. In the foreground, a stalled car that could not make it through the flood awaits rescue.

Department arrived and rescued them. When the firefighters learned about Williams's stepfather, they searched for him, too. His body was finally found a week after the storm.

THE TOWN THAT REFUSED TO DISAPPEAR

Princeville, North Carolina, is widely believed to be the oldest all-African American town in the United States. Hurricane Floyd challenged its residents like never before. Located next to the Tar River, the town flooded when the dike protecting it burst in seven places. It was perhaps the hardest-hit community during Floyd.

Anne Howell, one of the town's commissioners, recalled to National Public Radio the events of that night. Her cousin and brother-in-law, trying to sandbag the dike, called and told her, "You better get your people out of there! We can't hold the water back." Howell and a friend started banging on neighbors' windows and doors. The people that they warned barely had time to get out before the water came. Crashing through the windows of houses and tipping over trailers, the waters reached as high as 30 feet (9 m) in some places.

Howell and others gathered on high ground at a nearby parking lot. She recalled families holding on to one another, many crying. Howell turned to a local police officer, asking him what had become of Princeville. He paused before he told her, "I hate to tell you this, but there is no more Princeville."

The devastation to Princeville was so great that it became a ghost town after the hurricane. The Federal Emergency Management Agency (FEMA) offered to buy out the entire area for the federal government, or to rebuild the dike, but not both. The town was torn: many residents wanted to move elsewhere. But many others, including Howell, refused to leave. The commission voted to stay and rebuild.

It took years, but Princeville came back. Even now, however, Howell cannot shake the memory of the destruction.

Anne Howell, a Princeville town commissioner, stands on the deck of her home, which was destroyed by Hurricane Floyd's floods.

THE AFTERMATH

By the time the waters had receded, Hurricane Floyd had flooded 63,000 homes in North Carolina, destroying 7,300 of them. The National Hurricane Center estimated that the storm caused $5.5 billion in damage. Fifty-two people lost their lives. Those who survived spent years rebuilding.

4

HURRICANE KATRINA

In August 2005, the United States suffered its worst natural disaster. Hurricane Katrina ravaged the Gulf Coast. Mississippi and Louisiana were the hardest hit, and the city of New Orleans experienced its greatest crisis in history.

Having caused nine deaths as a Category 1 storm in Florida on August 25, Katrina moved into the Gulf of Mexico. By 2 AM Sunday, Katrina intensified to Category 5, with winds of 175 mph (282 km/h). Mayor Ray Nagin ordered New Orleans' first-ever mandatory evacuation. Traffic slowed to a crawl as about 380,000 people fled the area. Still, approximately 100,000 people remained behind. Some did not have access to cars or ways of getting out. Others did not take the threat seriously. After all, many hurricane warnings had occurred over the years, with little real damage.

Similar evacuations were taking place along the Gulf. Between 4 and 7 AM on Monday, August 29, Katrina made landfall from Louisiana to Alabama. The 125 mph (201 km/h) winds and massive storm surge devastated the coast. About 90 percent of buildings on the coast from

Biloxi to Gulfport, Mississippi, were demolished. Many seaside towns were almost completely destroyed.

In New Orleans, about 10,000 people sought refuge at the Superdome, a sports stadium. Others hoped for the best and stayed in their homes. By Monday afternoon, Katrina had moved on. There had been great damage, but city residents and officials were relieved. They thought they had missed the full impact of the hurricane.

In a mandatory evacuation in advance of Hurricane Katrina, motorists leave New Orleans on August 28, 2005.

A City Submerged

The worst was actually yet to come. Much of New Orleans is below sea level, with protective walls, or levees, keeping out water from the Mississippi River and Lake Pontchartrain. The rains and storm surge had weakened these levees. When some of them failed, water started filling the city on Monday afternoon. By Tuesday evening, more than 80 percent of the city was flooded. The water reached as high as 20 feet (6 m) in many places.

An aerial view of submerged highways and neighborhood streets in flooded New Orleans on September 7, 2005, more than a week after Hurricane Katrina overwhelmed the city's levees and trapped thousands of residents.

Thousands of people were trapped as the waters rose quickly. They took refuge on roofs and in attics, or on dry patches of land. The Coast Guard made many of the early rescues. Police, emergency workers, and regular citizens rushed into action. Not enough help came when it was needed, however. Some people escaped the flood, but didn't have food or water. People grew desperate as they waited for help that was slow to appear. For days, thousands waited to be evacuated from the city's convention center.

The submerged and damaged streets made getting around extremely difficult. In addition, the hurricane and floods had wiped out the city's water and power. Means of communication were affected, making it hard for first responders to be in contact with one another and for victims to get hold of them. Katrina had paralyzed an entire city, and time was running out.

THREE DESPERATE DAYS

For one New Orleans family, the ordeal of Hurricane Katrina proved nearly unbearable. Debbie Este, who is wheelchair-bound, lived with two teenage daughters, Tiffany and Amanda, and her elderly mother. Like many, she didn't think the storm would be any worse than previous ones. The family also didn't want to leave their pets behind.

When the flood came, it was shockingly fast. In only a few minutes, they were submerged waist-deep on the first floor. The Estes grabbed their pets, and the girls helped their mother up the attic steps. Between them, they had only about a gallon (3.8 liters) of drinking water. The attic had no windows, and it became incredibly hot. The flooding continued to worsen. On the second day, it had reached the opening of the attic door. Hoping that noise would alert rescuers, the girls banged on the inside of the roof.

Debbie's sixty-eight-year-old mother had suffered from heart trouble months earlier. Between the heat and stress, she grew delirious. After a day and a half in the attic, she passed away. Distraught over the death of her mother and their situation, Debbie almost lost hope. The girls tried to boost their mother's spirits: Amanda talked about finishing school, finding a job, and getting married. Both of them kept telling her that they would make it out alive. Their drinking water soon ran out, however. By the third day, Wednesday, the floodwaters reached the attic.

When Debbie heard a voice outside the attic, she thought she was dreaming. Her brother and some friends had reached their house by boat. Screaming, "We're here!" they waited as Aldo Harrold chopped away at the roof. Eventually, there was an opening big enough for the three of them and their two dogs to make it out and onto the boat.

Recovering later at a Red Cross shelter, Debbie Este told a CNN reporter, "I'm in shock. I can't even think . . . I still keep blaming myself. I say we should have left." Este also feared for her brother. After he saved them, she had lost touch with him for days. When they finally spoke, "We were both crying. I knew he was all right . . . that made a big difference to me."

Two weeks later, Este and her daughters found temporary housing in South Carolina. Grateful to pick up the pieces of her life, she was still in a state of disbelief. "I feel like I'm halfway in a place of where I've been and where I'm going," she told CNN. "It took me a long time to accumulate what I had, and I've got to start over again. But I'm sure I'll make it."

The Call of Duty

Patrick Hartman was a New Orleans police officer. In the wake of Katrina, a third of the city's 1,740 officers could not—or did not—make it to work. Hartman had planned to help with the cleanup, but his plans changed dramatically when the city started flooding.

Hartman was getting ready for work when the 17th Street Canal levee broke. Water rushed through the alley next to his apartment, and in moments was waist-high. To escape, Hartman dove out into the water. He could not touch the ground and was barely able to swim in the rushing tide. He was carried from one house to another. Trying to enter one building, he attempted to break a window with his pocketknife. The knife slipped and Hartman cut himself. The powerful water continued to carry him away. Thankfully, however, he was able to grab onto a tree's branches. Seeing another house, he swam toward it. Barefoot and

New Orleans police officer Patrick Hartman balances on a windowsill during a search and rescue operation. It was one of many he would participate in after he himself barely escaped Katrina's flooding.

bleeding, Hartman made it through a window. Exhausted, he fell asleep upstairs in the abandoned house.

That night, Hartman tried waving a flashlight he had found at a passing helicopter, but the rescuers did not see him. By morning, the water in the house had risen to the first-floor ceiling. It was time to go. He wrote an apology note to the absent family for breaking into their house. When he noticed a man passing by in a boat, he smashed a window and swam toward the boat. Rather than go to safety and recover after being rescued, Hartman manned another boat. By nightfall, the policeman had rescued fifteen people from rooftops and porches.

Hartman dropped by his mother's house to let her know he was OK. He stayed just long enough to get a change of clothes. After that, he barely rested for a week. At one point, he and other officers battled snipers at a motel. Hartman also helped guide U.S. Marines through the submerged city on search and rescue missions.

Like many officers and emergency workers, Hartman had lost all he owned. He admitted he felt betrayed by those who had not shown up for work. Some may have been rescuing their families or unable to make it in. In the weeks following, fifty-two police officers would be fired for desertion. A few dozen turned in their badges. For Hartman, however, and for thousands of others, quitting was not an option.

Caught by the Surge

In Mississippi, the unstoppable rush of seawater was the greatest danger. Witnesses reported storm surges of 20 to 30 feet (6 to 9 m) high. Flooding affected areas as far as 6 miles (10 km) inland. Katrina left buildings piled on top of each other, flattened by the storm's sheer force. In Gulfport, residents who stayed were caught off guard. "I antici-pated it being bad, but not nearly as severe as it turned out," beachfront resident Mike Spencer told NBC's "Today" show. He decided to stay when his neighbors said they would not evacuate. "That kind of gave

me the courage . . . or the stupidity to go ahead and stay out, too."
He realized too late that he had misjudged Katrina's impact. His
house began filling with water. The water got so high that he fled to
the attic. With no other way out, he started kicking the wall. Slowly,
he made a hole large enough to squeeze through. Luckily, he discovered that there was a tree just outside the wall.

Climbing into the tree, for five hours Spencer watched nearby homes
vanish. He tried to keep his spirits up and thought, "Eventually, it's going

Gulfport, Mississippi, residents Anne Anderson and Vernon Lacour, shown
here in an interview on NBC's "Today" show, tell how they discovered
next-door neighbor, Mike Spencer *(left)* in a tree, hours after escaping the
storm surge that flooded his coastal home.

to be over and I'll be here to enjoy this morning." His neighbors Anne Anderson and Vernon Lacour found him when they came back to check on their house, which was also gone. Anderson had lived there for decades and was heartbroken by the loss. Still, she told NBC, "The bottom line is, family means everything. And I have got my father and my husband. And so, really, in a big way, I'm blessed."

A Region Mourns and Recovers

Months after the hurricane, the true death toll is unknown. More than 1,300 deaths in Louisiana and 230 in Mississippi have been confirmed. Hundreds more are still missing. Less than half of the 450,000 people who lived in New Orleans have returned. Those who lost their homes have been scattered around the country, many of them nearby in Houston, Texas, and Baton Rouge, Louisiana. Whole parts of New Orleans are still vacant, but people are slowly trickling back in.

In Mississippi, the recovery has been quicker. The water that flooded its coast quickly disappeared, while New Orleans was underwater for weeks. Still, 36,000 families live in temporary trailers. Towns that were completely destroyed remain largely empty.

For the survivors of New Orleans, the future brings both hope and uncertainty. Those who return have a long road ahead of them, but they are determined to restore the city's unique character. New Orleans, for better or for worse, is a city forever changed by Katrina.

GLOSSARY

bunker An enclosed shelter that protects its occupants from an outside danger.

debris Bits of objects that remain after destructive events.

disaster A man-made or natural event causing widespread destruction.

eye In relation to a hurricane, a relatively calm area in the center of the storm.

Federal Emergency Management Agency (FEMA) The department of the federal government responsible for reacting to natural disasters and other emergencies.

first responders Emergency workers such as firefighters and police officers, who are among the first to help those in danger.

ground zero The location of the greatest impact or destruction during a disaster.

hurricane A powerful tropical storm that brings strong winds, heavy rain, and, usually, a rise in sea level. To be considered a hurricane, a storm must have sustained winds of at least 74 mph (119 km/h).

hurricane warning A warning that a hurricane is likely to hit a specific area within twenty-four hours.

hurricane watch A warning that a storm may develop into a hurricane within thirty-six hours.

landfall The time and/or location when the eye of a hurricane reaches a coastline.

landslide The downward motion or sliding of a mass of earth and rock.

levee A barrier constructed to prevent a river or other body of water from flooding. Also known as a dike.

meteorologist A person who studies the science of weather.

National Hurricane Center (NHC) The branch of the U.S. National Weather Service located in Miami, Florida, that is in charge of tracking tropical storms and hurricanes and providing information on them to the government and the media.

Saffir-Simpson Hurricane Scale The ranking of hurricanes by intensity from Category 1 to Category 5 storms, from weakest to strongest.

search and rescue workers Emergency workers (usually trained) who look for lost, injured, trapped, or otherwise endangered victims.

storm surge A rise in the level of ocean water—caused mainly by a hurricane's powerful winds—that can threaten coastal areas.

tornado A violently rotating and destructive column of air ranging in size from a few yards to a mile wide.

tropical storm A weather disturbance in which sustained winds are at least 39 mph (63 km/h), but are less than 74 mph (119 km/h). It is the precursor to a hurricane.

FOR MORE INFORMATION

The American Red Cross
2025 E Street NW
Washington, DC 20006
(202) 303-4498
Web site: http://www.redcross.org

Canadian Hurricane Centre
Environment Canada
45 Alderney Drive
Dartmouth, NS B2Y 2N6
Canada
(902) 426-7231
Web site: http://www.atl.ec.gc.ca/weather/hurricane/index_e.html

Federal Emergency Management Agency (FEMA)
500 C Street SW
Washington, DC 20472
(800) 621-FEMA (3362)
Web site: http://www.fema.gov

National Hurricane Center (NHC)
11691 SW 17th Street

Miami, FL 33165-2149

Web site: http://www.nhc.noaa.gov

National Search and Rescue Secretariat

400-275 Slater Street

Ottawa, ON K1A 0K2

Canada

(800) 727-9414

Web site: http://www.nss.gc.ca/site/index_e.asp

The USA Freedom Corps

1600 Pennsylvania Avenue NW

Washington, DC 20500

(877) USA-CORP (872-2677)

Web site: http://www.usafreedomcorps.gov

Web Sites

Due to the changing nature of Internet links, Rosen Publishing has developed an online list of Web sites related to the subject of this book. This site is updated regularly. Please use this link to access the list:

http://www.rosenlinks.com/ss/hurr

FOR FURTHER READING

Ceban, Bonnie J. *Hurricanes, Typhoons, and Cyclones: Disaster & Survival* (Deadly Disasters). Berkeley Heights, NJ: Enslow Publishers, 2005.

Chambers, Catherine. *Hurricanes* (Disasters in Nature). Portsmouth, NH: Heinemann, 2000.

Dixon, Dougal, and Neil Morris. *Hurricane Destruction.* Columbus, OH: Waterbird Press, 2004.

Green, Jen. *Hurricane Andrew* (Disasters). Milwaukee, WI: Gareth Stevens Publishing, 2005.

Miller, Debra A. *Hurricane Katrina: Devastation on the Gulf Coast.* San Diego, CA: Lucent Books, 2006.

Nicolson, Cynthia Pratt. *Hurricane!* (Disaster). Tonawanda, NY: Kids Can Press, 2002.

Parks, Peggy J. *Hurricanes* (Kidhaven Science Library). San Diego, CA: Blackbirch Press, 2006.

BIBLIOGRAPHY

Allen, Diane Lacey. "The Story of Three Families." *Pyschology Today*, November 1992.

Associated Press. "Katrina Aftermath Taking Toll on Police." CNN.com. September 13, 2005. Retrieved April 2006 (http://www.cnn.com/2005/US/09/04/katrina.police.ap/index.html).

Barnes, Jay. *Florida's Hurricane History.* Chapel Hill, NC: The University of North Carolina Press, 1998.

Barnes, Jay. *North Carolina's Hurricane History.* Chapel Hill, NC: The University of North Carolina Press, 2001.

Bennett, Brian. "On the Forgotten Coast." Time.com. September 15, 2005. Retrieved April 2006 (http://www.time.com/time/nation/article/0,8599,1105526,00.html).

Brunker, Mike. "Survivors Tell of Desperate Struggles to Survive." MSNBC.com. August 30, 2005. Retrieved April 2006 (http://www.msnbc.msn.com/id/9129659).

Chase, Randall. "Hurricane Brings Tragedy to N.C. Family, Friends." *The Topeka Capital-Journal*, September 20, 1999.

Davies, Pete. *Inside the Hurricane: Face to Face with Nature's Deadliest Storms.* New York, NY: Henry Holt and Company, 2006.

Loyn, David. "Americas Mitch Survivor: My Six-Day Ordeal." BBCNews.co.uk. November 9, 1998. Retrieved April 2006 (http://news.bbc.co.uk/1/hi/world/americas/210769.stm).

Manegold, Catherine S. "Hurricane Andrew: Amid Wreckage, Survivors Tell Their Stories." *New York Times*, August 25, 1992.

McKinley, James C., Jr. "The Hurricane Is History, but for Battered Honduras the Agony Lingers." *New York Times*, December 25, 1998.

McKinley, James C., Jr. "Still Locked in Storm's Horror, Hondurans Are Fearful of Future." *New York Times*, January 17, 1999.

Moore, Richard, and Jay Barnes. *Faces from the Flood: Hurricane Floyd Remembered.* Chapel Hill, NC: The University of North Carolina Press, 2004.

Pangyanszki, Jennifer. "New Start for Family That Survived 3 Days in Attic." CNN.com. September 12, 2005. Retrieved April 2006 (http://www.cnn.com/2005/US/09/12/katrina.survivors.folo/index.html).

Pangyanszki, Jennifer. "3 Days of Death, Despair and Survival." CNN.com. September 9, 2005. Retrieved April 2006 (http://www.cnn.com/2005/US/09/09/katrina.survivors).

Pittman, Craig. "Storm's Howl Fills the Ears of Survivors." St. *Petersburg Times*, August 18, 2002. Retrieved April 2006 (http://www.sptimes.com/2002/webspecials02/andrew/day1/story1.shtml).

Yellin, Emily. "Town with Fabled Past Facing Uncertain Future." *New York Times*, November 22, 1999.

Zucchino, David. "New Orleans Police Officer Made the Flood His Beat." *Seattle Times*, September 28, 2005.

INDEX

ABOUT THE AUTHOR

Philip Wolny is a writer and editor living in New York. Though his own experiences with inclement weather have been limited to unbearable humidity and the occasional snow day, he has always had a great interest in—and profound respect for—the power of Mother Nature. He hopes that this book will give readers insight into the triumph of the spirit of coastal dwellers who have braved these fierce storms.

PHOTO CREDITS

Photo credits: Cover © Mario Tama/Getty Images; p. 4 Jacques Descloitres, MODIS Rapid Response Team, NASA/GSFC; p. 6 © Todd Bigelow/ Aurora/Getty Images; p. 10 © Robert Sullivan/AFP/Getty Images; p. 11 Courtesy Stan Goldenberg; pp. 13, 20 © AP/Wide World Photos; p. 17 © Yann Arthus-Bertrand/ Corbis, (inset) Courtesy Don Pearly; p. 22 © Yuri Cortez/AFP/Getty Images; p. 26 Courtesy Naval Aviation News; p. 27 © Justin Lane/Liaison Agency/Getty Images; p. 29 © Greg Halpern; p. 31 © James Nielsen/AFP/Getty Images; p. 22 Jocelyn Augustino/FEMA; p. 36 Robert Gauthier/Los Angeles Times; p. 38 NBC News Archives.

Designer: Tahara Anderson; Editor: Elizabeth Gavril
Photo Researcher: Amy Feinberg